Contents

Welcome

1 Listen to the story. Read.

1

People on Earth are sick. Everyone has got tickilitis.

Sad news, Captain Conrad. Can we help?

2

Have you got a tifftiff plant? It is the only medicine for tickilitis.

Yes, we've got tifftiff plants on Space Island.

3

The tifftiff plant is a medicine. It's very important.

4

Please come to Space Island. We can help you find a tifftiff plant.

Thank you!

Can understand a simple story

Can understand a simple story

2 🎧 1:03 **Listen, tick (✓) and say.**

3 🎧 1:04 / 1:05 **Listen and sing. Then find the tifftiff plant.**

Hey boys! Hey girls!
Come with us to Space Island.
Look up, down, here, there.
Look around everywhere.
Where's the tifftiff plant?
Come on, come on,
Let's find the tifftiff plant!

WELCOME TO SPACE ISLAND

I'm President Pop.
Welcome to Space Island.

Hello. I'm Captain Conrad.

My name's Katy.

I'm eight.

How old are you, Katy?

I'm Kim.
I'm nine.

I'm PROD 1.

And I'm PROD 2!
Hello!

4 🎧 1:06 **Listen and chant.**

a A, b B, c C, d D, e E, f F, g G, h H, i I, j J,
k K, l L, m M, n N, o O, p P, q Q, r R, s S,
t T, u U, v V, w W, xX, y Y, z Z

Can name characters in a story / Can say the alphabet

5 Listen and say. Then circle the characters' favourite numbers.

21 twenty-one	**22** twenty-two	**23** twenty-three	**24** twenty-four	**25** twenty-five
26 twenty-six	**27** twenty-seven	**28** twenty-eight	**29** twenty-nine	**30** thirty
31 thirty-one	**32** thirty-two	**33** thirty-three	**34** thirty-four	**35** thirty-five
36 thirty-six	**37** thirty-seven	**38** thirty-eight	**39** thirty-nine	**40** forty
41 forty-one	**42** forty-two	**43** forty-three	**44** forty-four	**45** forty-five
46 forty-six	**47** forty-seven	**48** forty-eight	**49** forty-nine	**50** fifty

6 Listen and say.

Monday   Tuesday   Wednesday
Thursday   Friday   Saturday
Sunday

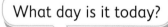
What day is it today?

It's Thursday.

7   How do you spell it?

1 Nature

sun

birds

1 ⭐ **What do you know?**

2 🎧 1:10 **Listen and find. What's missing?**

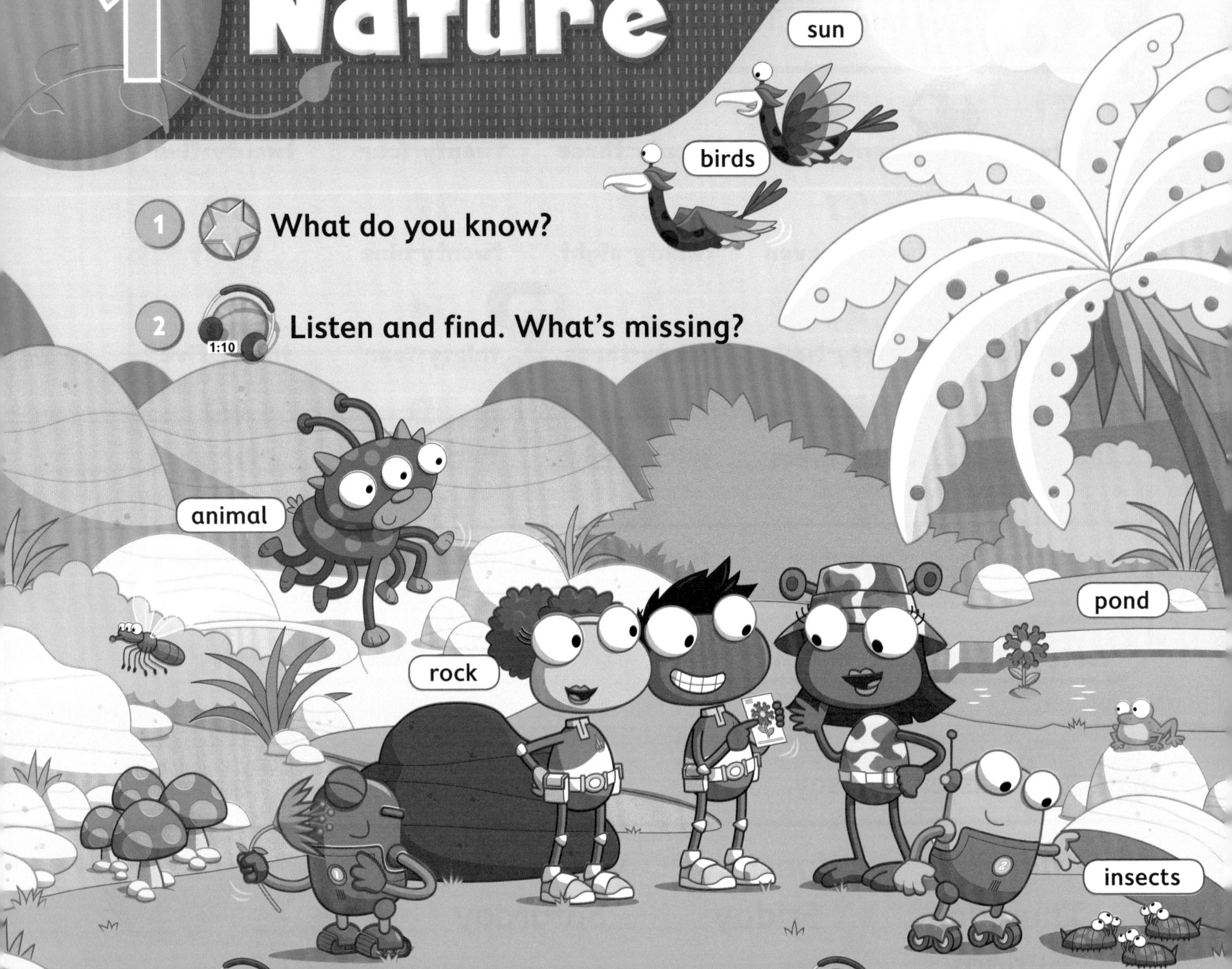

animal

rock

pond

insects

3 🎧 1:11 **Listen and number.**

4 🎧 1:12 **Listen and say.**

a [ ]

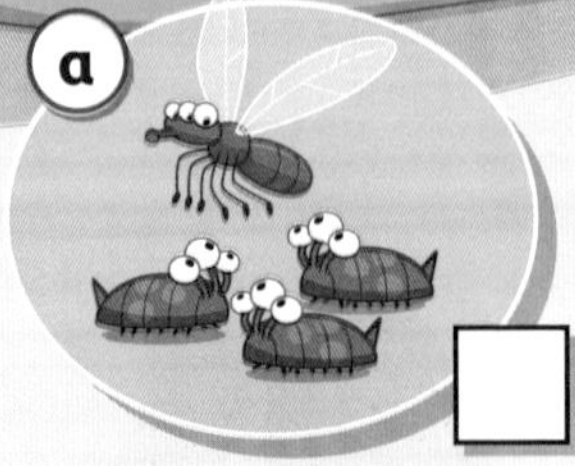

b [ ]

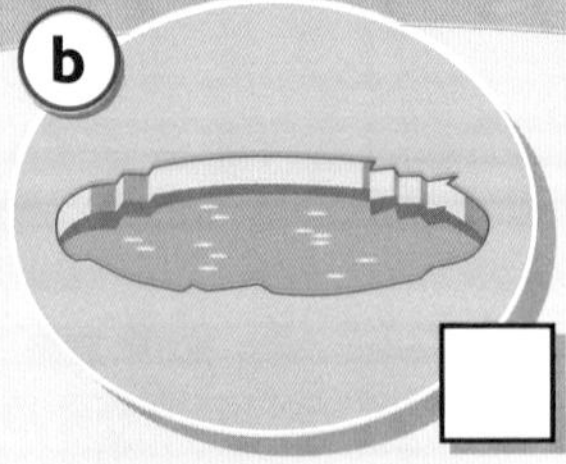

c [ ]

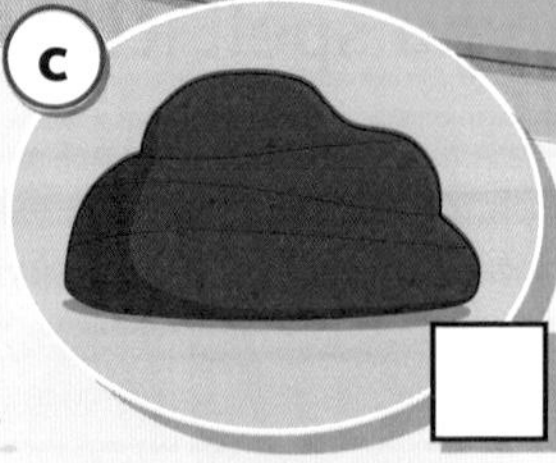

d [ ]

e [ ]

f [ ]

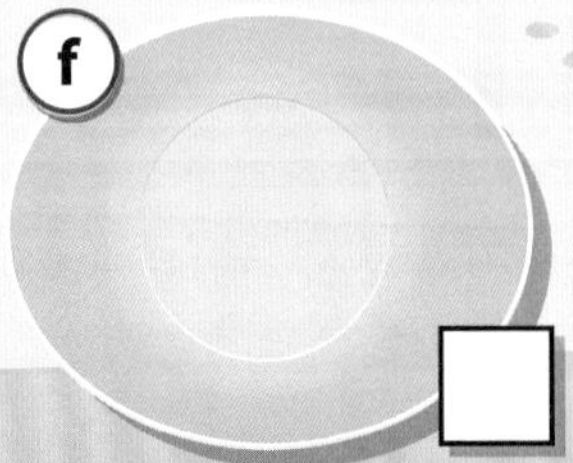

g [ ]

Can identify some common nature words

flowers

5 **Listen and chant.
Circle the nature words.**

There's a pond, a blue pond.
There's a rock, a brown rock.
There's an animal, a purple animal.

There are birds, blue birds.
There are insects, pink insects.
There are flowers, yellow flowers.

LOOK!

1:14

There is	a blue pond.
There's	
There are	pink insects.

6 **Play a memory game.**

> There's a purple animal.

> There are two birds.

Listen and sing.

1:16 / 1:17

How many birds are there?
There are seven birds.
There are six mushrooms.
There are five rocks.
Seven, six, five,
Stamp, stamp, stamp!
How many animals are there?
There are four animals.
There are three trees.

There are two clouds.
Four, three, two,
Clap, clap, clap!
How many ponds are there?
There's one pond.
One blue pond.
Only one blue pond,
Jump, jump, splash!

 trees

clouds

 mushrooms

 **LOOK!**

1:18

| How many ponds are there? | There's one pond. |
| How many birds are there? | There are seven birds. |

8  **Ask and answer.**

How many birds are there?

There are seven birds.

9 Look, read and say the title.

There's a butterfly. There are black birds. There are three trees. They are green.

① **Three big ducks**

② **Three red balls**

③ *Three green trees*

10 1:19 Now listen and check.

11 1:20 Listen and say.

SOUNDS FUN!

Trees, trees, trees.
Green, green trees.
Three green trees.
Lee sees
Three green trees.

12 Play the game.

There's a tree.

Yes.

Talk about the pictures. Then listen and read.

14 **Act out the story.**

15 What do you know?

16 **Count and write. Then listen and check your answers.**
1:24

+ (plus)   − (minus)   = (equals)

1   +   = ☐

2   −   = ☐

3   +  = ☐

4   −   = ☐

17 **Read the number puzzles. Then write the answer.**

1 Three birds plus one spider. How many legs? ☐

2 Two insects minus one cat. How many legs? ☐

 PROJECT

**Make an insect.
Talk to a friend.**

1 **Think** about insects.
2 **Choose** an insect.
3 **Make** an insect.
4 **Talk** about your insect.

18 **Listen and number.**

a  ☐

b  ☐

c  ☐

d  ☐

e  ☐

f  ☐

g  ☐

h  ☐

19 **Play a guessing game. Ask and answer.**

There are two trees.

Picture g?

No. There are five birds.

Picture d!

20 **Draw the view from your window in your notebook. Talk to a friend.**

There's a big cloud.

There are three trees.

 **I CAN**

I can identify some common nature words.

I can talk about how many there are.

I can do simple sums and number puzzles.

Can assess what I have learnt in Unit 1

21 **Spot the differences. Cover a picture. Talk to a friend.** **HAVE FUN**

A

B

There's a pond in my picture.

There's a pond in my picture, too.

There are three rocks.

No! There are four rocks!

Now go to Poptropica English World

Lesson 8

Can use what I have learnt in Unit 1

13

Wider World 1

Birthdays around the world

1 What do you know?

2 Listen and read. How old is Yoon-ji?

1

Hi, I'm Lucy. I'm from the USA. Today is my birthday. I'm nine. Look at my birthday cake. There are nine candles. My friends and family sing 'Happy Birthday' and I blow out the candles. I love birthdays!

candle

cake

2

piñata

My name's Diego and I'm eight. I'm from Mexico. Look! It's my birthday party. There's a big *piñata* with sweets inside. We break the *piñata* and the sweets fall out.

Can understand texts about other children's birthdays

banchan

seaweed soup

Hello. I'm Yoon-ji and I'm from Korea. I'm eight today. For my birthday, I have a big breakfast in the morning with seaweed soup and a lot of different dishes called *banchan*. Yum!

 Read and circle.

1   Diego's (eight / nine).

2   There are (nine / ten) candles on Lucy's cake.

3   There are (sweets / cakes) in the *piñata*.

4   Yoon-ji likes (cake / soup) on her birthday.

 Ask and answer.

1   How old are you?

2   Is there a cake at your birthday party?

3   Are there candles?

4   Is there a piñata?

5   Are there sweets?

Tell the Class

2 Me

2 🎧 1:27 Listen and find. What's missing?

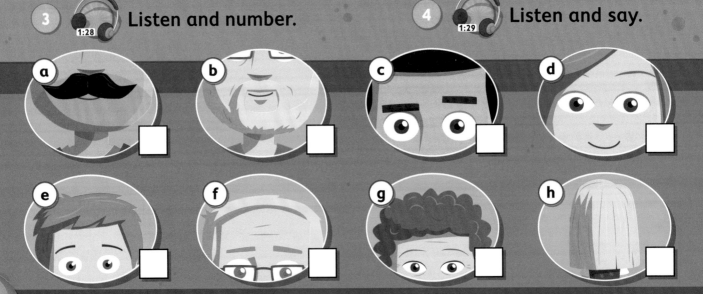

blonde hair

brown eyes

grey hair

glasses

a black moustache

blue eyes

a short beard

red hair

Peter

Jane

3 🎧 1:28 Listen and number.

4 🎧 1:29 Listen and say.

a ☐

b ☐

c ☐

d ☐

e ☐

f ☐

g ☐

h ☐

Can identify some physical characteristics

5 Listen and chant. Who has got brown eyes?

I've got black hair.
I've got brown eyes.
I haven't got glasses.
Look, it's Dad!

She's got brown hair.
She's got brown eyes.
She hasn't got glasses.
Look, it's Granny!

LOOK!

1:32

I	've got	glasses.
	haven't got	a short beard.
He She	's got	blonde hair.
	hasn't got	

6 Play a guessing game.

He's got red hair.
He hasn't got glasses.

Peter!

Can describe people's physical characteristics

7 **Listen and sing.** 1:33 / 1:34

Who is it? Who is it?
Who is it?

Have you got long hair?
Yes, I have. (x3)
Have you got a small nose?
Yes, I have.
Have you got red hair?
No, I haven't. (x3)
Have you got green eyes?
Yes, I have.
Have you got a long neck?
Yes, I have. (x3)
Have you got big teeth?
Yes, I have.

nose

teeth

neck

a

b

c

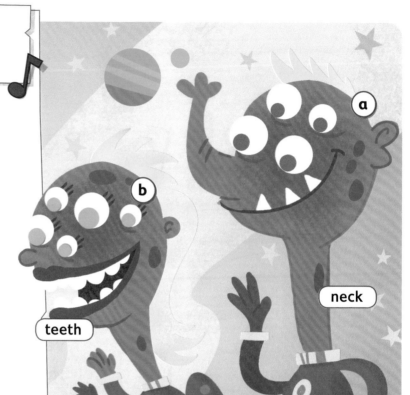

LOOK! 1:35

| **Have** you **got** | a long neck? | Yes, I **have**. |
| | a big nose? | No, I **haven't**. |

  8 **Ask and answer.**

Have you got
long hair?

No, I haven't.

HOME SCHOOL LINK

Listen and number.

Mike

Bob

Sharon

 **Listen and check.**

11 **Listen and say.**

SOUNDS FUN!

Sharon's got **sh**ort hair.
She's got **sh**ort, **sh**ort hair.

12 **Play the game.**

He's got a big nose.

He's got red hair.

He's got glasses.

Lesson 4 Can listen to and talk about people's physical characteristics / Can pronounce words that include /ʃ/

19

Talk about the pictures. Then listen and read.

14 **Act out the story.**

Can understand a simple story / Can act out a story

15 **What do you know?**

16 1:43 **Listen and read. Which animal has got a long tail?**

Australian animals

pouch

The kangaroo has got a big body and a pouch. It's got two long legs and two short arms. It's got a long tail and big feet. It's got a small head. It's got big ears and small eyes.

feathers

This bird is an emu. It's got a big body and two wings with long feathers. It's got two long legs. It's got a long neck and a small head. It's got big eyes.

17 1:44 **Listen and answer. *True* or *false*?**

18 **Choose an animal and describe it to your friend.**

koala
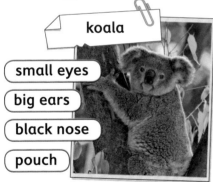

 small eyes
big ears
black nose
 pouch

The koala has got...

PROJECT

**Make a poster.
Talk to a friend.**

wombat

small eyes
small ears
brown fur
short legs

The wombat has got...

1 **Think** about animals in your country.
2 **Choose** some animals.
3 **Make** a poster of animals in your country.
4 **Talk** about your poster.

19 **Read and tick (✓).**

(1)

(2)

(3)

1 glasses ☐
a big nose ☐
a beard ☐

2 a beard ☐
a red nose ☐
a moustache ☐

3 a red nose ☐
grey hair ☐
glasses ☐

20 **Listen and tick (✓).**

(1) ⓐ  ☐ ⓑ  ☐ ⓒ  ☐

(2) ⓐ  ☐ ⓑ  ☐ ⓒ  ☐

(3) ⓐ  ☐ ⓑ  ☐

(4) ⓐ  ☐ ⓑ  ☐

21 **Look at Activity 20. Talk to a friend.**

He's got short black hair. He hasn't got a moustache.

Picture 3a!

I can identify some physical characteristics.

I can describe people's physical characteristics.

I can understand short texts about Australian animals.

22 **Choose. Then play.**

① Jonas

② Jenny

③ Bill

④ Susan

⑤ Marco

⑥ David

⑦ Alice

⑧ Joe

⑨ Peter

⑩ Lucy

⑪ Adam

⑫ Rosie

⑬ Jack

⑭ Julie

⑮ Sally

⑯ Betty

Have you got brown hair?

Yes, I have.

Have you got a moustache?

Yes, I have.

Are you Bill?

Yes!

 **Now go to Poptropica English World**

3 Pets

1 ⭐ **What do you know?**

2 🎧 1:46 **Listen and find. What's missing?**

 cat

 frog

 parrot

 fish

 rabbit

 snake

 dog

3 🎧 1:47 **Listen and number.**   4 🎧 1:48 **Listen and say.**

a  ☐

b 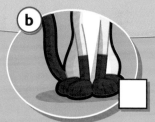 ☐

c  ☐

d 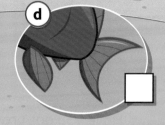 ☐

e  ☐

f 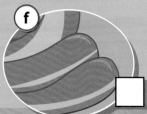 ☐

g  ☐

Can identify some pets

5 1:50 **Listen and chant. Circle the animal.**

Has it got two eyes?
Yes, it has.
Has it got four legs?
No, it hasn't.
Has it got a tail?
Yes, it has.
Has it got two hands?
No, it hasn't.
Splish, splash, splish,
It's a fish!

LOOK!
1:51

| Has it got four legs? | Yes, it **has**. |
| | No, it **hasn't**. |

6 **Look at the animals in Activity 5. Ask and answer.**

Has it got big eyes?

Yes, it has.

Pets, pets, pets are great fun!
There's a pet for everyone!

Have they got a tortoise?
Yes, they have!
It's got pretty eyes and ugly legs.
It's great fun!

Have they got a cat?
No, they haven't.
Have they got a dog?
No, they haven't.

Have they got a hamster?
Yes, they have!
It's got pretty eyes and a small nose.
It's great fun!

pretty

tortoise

ugly

hamster

LOOK! 1:54

| Have they got a cat? | Yes, they **have**. |
| | No, they **haven't**. |

8 **Ask and answer.**

Have they got a fish?

Yes, they have.

It's got pretty eyes and a tail.

 HOME SCHOOL LINK

9   **Look and read. How old is Boris?**

Animal:	Tarantula
Name:	Boris
Home:	Arizona
Age:	3 years old
Legs:	Brown, 8 legs. Hair. Ugly
Food:	Likes insects

Hi, I'm Alex and I've got a pet. It's a tarantula. Its name is Boris and it's from Arizona. It's three years old. It's brown. It hasn't got a tail. It's got eight legs and hair. It's really ugly and it likes insects!

10 1:56 **Listen and answer.**

SOUNDS FUN!

11 1:57 **Listen and say.**

The cat looks at the rat.
The rat looks at the snake.
The snake looks at the cake.

12 **Play the game.**

It's got long ears.

Is it a rabbit?

1

The trickster has got the wabberjock! Please help me!

2

What does the wabberjock look like?

It's got a long tail.

3

Has it got sharp teeth?

No, it hasn't.

4

Is it very big?

No, it's small.

5

Is it the wabberjock?!

Ooooh! It's beautiful!

6

You've got the wabberjock!

Hurray!

14   **Act out the story.**

Can understand a simple story / Can act out a story

15 What do you know?

16 **1:61** Listen and read. Then match.

a

butterflies

c

eggs

1 First, there are small eggs.
2 Next, there are caterpillars. They've got a lot of legs.
3 Then there are cocoons.
4 Finally, there are butterflies. They've got wings with many colours. They're pretty.

b

cocoons

d

caterpillars

17 **1:62** Listen and read. Then answer.

First, there are small eggs in the water.

Then the tadpoles are big. They've got two legs now and long tails. They can swim fast.

Next, there are small tadpoles. They've got long tails. They haven't got legs.

Finally, there are young frogs. They've got four legs now. They've got big eyes and big mouths. They can jump.

 **PROJECT**

1 Where are the eggs?

2 Have small tadpoles got short tails?

3 Have big tadpoles got four legs?

4 What can frogs do?

Make a butterfly life cycle wheel. Talk to a friend.

1 **Think** about the life cycle of a butterfly.
2 **Prepare** and draw each stage.
3 **Make** a butterfly life cycle wheel.
4 **Talk** about the butterfly life cycle.

18 **Listen and number.**

 a

 b

 c

 d

 e

 f

 g

19 **Play a guessing game. Ask and answer.**

Has it got grey fur?

No, it hasn't.

Has it got wings?

Yes, it has.

Picture 3!

20 **Draw a pet in your notebook. Ask and answer.**

Have you got a pet?

Yes, I have. I've got a dog.

What does it look like?

It's got brown fur. It's got long ears and a long tail.

 I CAN

I can identify some pets.

I can talk about pets.

I can understand short texts about animal life cycles.

Can assess what I have learnt in Unit 3

21   **Draw pets in your house. Play the game.**

HAVE FUN

My house

garden

bathroom	bedroom 2
dining room	kitchen
bedroom 1	living room

garden

My friend's house

garden

bathroom	bedroom 2
dining room	kitchen
bedroom 1	living room

garden

There's a pet in the bathroom.

Has it got legs?

No, it hasn't.

Is it a snake?

Yes, it is.

Now go to Poptropica English World

Lesson 8

Can use what I have learnt in Unit 3

Wider World 2

Do you like pets?

1 **What do you know?**

2 **Listen and read. How many pets like fruit?**

> My name's Dagang. I'm from China. I've got a pet rabbit. His name's Baobao. He's white and he's got long ears. He doesn't like nuts. He likes apples and salad. I love my pet rabbit.

hamster wheel

> My name's Rika and I'm from Japan. I've got a pet hamster. Her name's Momo. She's two years old. She's got small ears and a small tail. She likes apples and nuts. She can run fast in the hamster wheel. She's so pretty. I love hamsters!

Can understand texts about other children's pets

(3)

I'm Pedro and I'm from Colombia. I've got a pet cat. Her name's Polly and she's nine years old. She's white. She likes fish and cheese but she doesn't like fruit. I love Polly.

(3) **Match.**

1   The rabbit

2   The hamster

3   The cat

a   likes fish and cheese.

b   likes apples and nuts.

c   likes apples and salad.

(4)  **Ask and answer.**

parrot

iguana

duck

spider

1   Do you like these pets?

2   Why do you like them?

3   What's your favourite pet?

Tell the class

4 Home

 1 ⭐ **What do you know?**

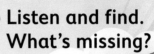 2 🎧 2:01 **Listen and find. What's missing?**

cooker

kitchen

shower

sofa

living room

TV

bedroom

 3 🎧 2:02 **Listen and match.**

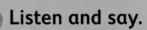 4 🎧 2:03 **Listen and say.**

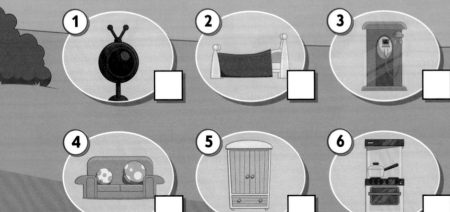

1 2 3 a b

4 5 6 c d

 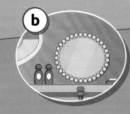  

Can identify rooms and some furniture

 5 2:04 **Listen and chant. Is the shower in the bedroom?**

Is the cooker in the kitchen?
Yes, it is. Yes, it is.

Is the sofa in the bedroom?
No, it isn't. No, no, no!

Is the shower in the bathroom?
Yes, it is. Yes, it is.

Is the bed in the living room?
No, it isn't. No, no, no.

 **LOOK!**
2:05

| **Is** the cooker **in** the kitchen? | Yes, it **is**. |
| | No, it **isn't**. |

6 2:06 **Listen and say. Then listen and answer.**

1   Is the cooker in the kitchen?

2   Is the TV in the bathroom?

3   Is the bed in the bedroom?

4   Is the shower in the living room?

Yes, it is.

7 **Ask and answer.**

Is the sofa in the bedroom?

No, it isn't.

8   2:07 / 2:08 **Listen and sing.**

 SONG

Animals, animals everywhere,
With animals here and animals there,
In, on, under, there.
Animals, animals everywhere.

Where's the frog?
It's in the bath.
In the bath?
That's a laugh!

Where's the snake?
It's on the chair.
On the chair?
Oh! Take care!

Where's the hamster?
It's under the lamp.
Under the lamp?
Turn, jump, stamp!

lamp

bath

chair

under

on

in

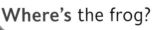 LOOK! 2:09

| Where's the frog? | It's in the bath. |

9 **Ask and answer.**

Where's the snake?

It's on the chair.

 HOME SCHOOL LINK

Can identify more furniture words / Can ask and answer about where things are

10 **Look and read. Why is Molly happy?**

Hi, I'm Molly. I'm very happy. My best friend is coming to my house! I've got a great new bed for her. It's cool! Where's the bed? In my bedroom. It's fantastic! It's green and it's got a picture of a frog on it. Where's the frog? It's in the pool. The bed is fun! Do you like it?

11  **Listen and answer.**
What is new in Molly's bedroom?

SOUNDS FUN!

12  **Listen and say.**

A hot dog in the school!
It's hot!

A cool frog in the pool!
It's cool!

13 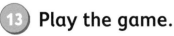 **Play the game.**

Is the bed under the cooker?

Yes, it is.

Talk about the pictures. Then listen and read.

1
Let's go and see Fid.

Fid's got a lot of plants. He can help us.

2
Have you got a tifftiff plant?

Yes, it's on the table.

3
Help!

Oh, no! The trickster has got the tifftiff plant!

4
Quick, the trickster is in the garden!

Oh, no, my beautiful house!

5
It isn't your plant. It's our plant!

Aaarrggh!

Phew!

6
Watch out! It's another trickster!

Oh, no. My kitchen!

  Act out the story.

Can understand a simple story / Can act out a story

16 **What do you know?**

17 **Read. Then listen and answer.**

2:16

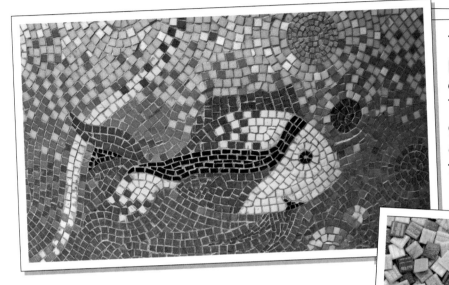

This is a mosaic. A mosaic is a picture with small tiles, stones or glass. They are very pretty. This is a picture of a fish. It's got squares, circles, rectangles and triangles in a lot of colours. Do you like mosaics?

tiles

stones

glass

18  **Count the shapes and write.**

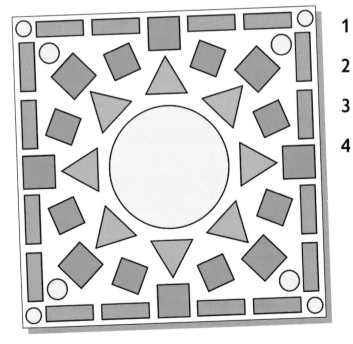

1 How many triangles are there? ☐

2 How many squares are there? ☐

3 How many circles are there? ☐

4 How many rectangles are there? ☐

**Make a mosaic picture.
Talk to a friend.**

1 **Think** about a subject for a mosaic.
2 **Prepare** and draw a mosaic.
3 **Make** a mosaic.
4 **Talk** about your mosaic.

19 **Look, read and tick (✓) or cross (✗).**

1   There's a duck in the bath.   ☐

2   There's a shower in the bathroom.   ☐

3   There's a cat under the bed in the bedroom.   ☐

4   There's a TV in the living room.   ☐

5   There's a table in the kitchen.   ☐

6   There's a cake on the cooker.   ☐

20  **Play a memory game. Ask and answer.**

Where's the plant?   It's on the table.

21 **Draw your bedroom. Ask and answer.**

 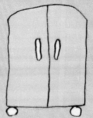

Where's the lamp?

It's on the table.

 I CAN

I can identify rooms and some furniture.
I can talk about where things are.
I can understand a text about a mosaic.

Spot the differences. Talk to a friend.

In picture A, there's a snake on the chair.

In picture B, the snake is under the chair.

Now go to Poptropica English World

Lesson 8

Can use what I have learnt in Unit 4

41

5 Clothes

1 ⭐ **What do you know?**

2 🎧 2:17 **Listen and find. What's missing?**

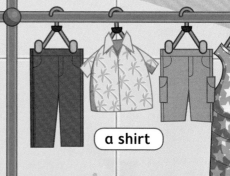
a shirt

shorts

a tracksuit

a cap

a uniform

a jacket

trainers

3 🎧 2:18 **Listen and number.** 4 🎧 2:19 **Listen and say.**

a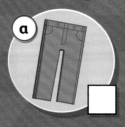

b

c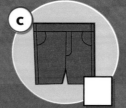

d

e

f

g

h

i

42 Lesson 1 Can identify some clothing items

jeans

a sweatshirt

5 2:21 **Listen and chant. Circle the clothes.**

Hey, hey! What are you wearing?
I'm wearing a uniform.
Hey, hey! What are you wearing?
I'm wearing a jacket.
PROD 2! What are you wearing?
I'm wearing a cap.
A cap?
It isn't a cap. It's a sweatshirt!

 2:22 **LOOK!**

| What **are** you **wearing**? | I'm wearing | a cap. |
| | | trainers. |

6 2:23 **Read and say.** *True* or *false?*
Listen and check.

1    I'm wearing a tracksuit.

2    I'm wearing a cap.

3    I'm wearing a sweatshirt.

7 **In pairs, talk about your clothes.**

What are you wearing?

I'm wearing jeans and a sweatshirt.

8   **Listen and sing.**

Where's my red scarf?
Where's my red scarf?
I've got my old blue jeans, my coat and my T-shirt,
But not my red scarf!
Not my red scarf!

My sister's in the bedroom.
What's she wearing?
She's wearing my socks.
Is she wearing my scarf?
No, she isn't, no, no, no!

My brother's in the garden.
What's he wearing?
He's wearing my trainers.
Is he wearing my scarf?
Yes, he is. Yes, yes, yes!

scarf

coat

socks

LOOK!
2:27

Is he/she wearing my scarf?	Yes, he/she is.
	No, he/she isn't.
What's he/she wearing?	He's/She's wearing socks.

9   **Ask and answer.**

Is he wearing white trainers?

Yes, he is.

Lesson 3   Can identify more clothing items

10 **Look and read. Is Ben wearing his favourite T-shirt?**

Fancy dress show

Hi, I'm Hilda. I'm a pirate! I'm wearing a black and red skirt. This is my favourite skirt. I'm wearing a white shirt, white socks and black shoes. These are my favourite shoes. Do you like my hat?

I'm Ben. I'm a clown! I'm wearing a big, yellow T-shirt and big, blue trousers. These are my favourite shoes. They are big and red. Do you like my orange hair?

11  **Listen and answer. *True* or *false*?**

SOUNDS FUN!

12  **Listen and say.**

Sky Skipper is wearing a short shirt and a short skirt.

13 **Play the game.**

I'm wearing jeans, a sweatshirt, trainers and a hat.

What are you wearing?

Talk about the pictures. Then listen and read.

1. The red trickster is here. He's got the tifftiff plant.

Let's find him.

2. Look at the red shirt!

Quick!

3. Look! It's the red trickster!

No, it's a red jacket.

4. You can't catch me!

5. Oh, no! This isn't a dress!

PROD 2 is wearing a dress. Ha!

6. Where's the tifftiff plant?

Oh, no! Look, it's up there!

  Act out the story.

Can understand a simple story / Can act out a story

16 **What do you know?**

17 **Listen, read and match.**
2:34

1

tidy the bedroom

make the bed

wash the dishes

lay the table

2

3

4

1 Mum: Help me lay the table, Amy.

  Amy: OK.

2 Dad: Can you tidy your bedroom, Donna?

  Donna: Yes, Dad.

3 Mum: Make the bed, please.

  Ann: Sorry. I can't. I'm busy.

4 Dad: Wash the dishes, Tom.

  Tom: OK.

18 **Look at Activity 17.**
2:35 **Listen and check.**

 **PROJECT**

Make a chores chart.
Talk to a friend.

1 **Think** about your chores this week.
2 **Prepare** a list of your chores.
3 **Make** a chores chart.
4 **Talk** about your chores chart.

19 **Listen and number.**

a    **b**    **c**

20 **Ask and answer the questions with a friend.**

Picture 1

1   Is she wearing yellow trousers?

2   Is she wearing big shoes?

Picture 2

3   Is she wearing a uniform?

4   Is she wearing black socks?

Picture 3

5   Is he wearing black trousers?

6   Is he wearing trainers?

21 **What are you wearing? Draw and write in your notebook. Ask and answer.**

What are you wearing?

I'm wearing a blue cap.

I can identify some clothing items.

I can talk about what people are wearing.

I can identify household chores.

22 **Choose. Then play.**

1
Rob

2
Beth

3
Harry

4
Suzy

5
Matt

6
Lulu

7
Tom

8
Nelly

9
Danny

It's a boy.

Is he wearing a scarf?

No, he isn't.

Is he wearing a cap?

Yes, he is.

It's Rob!

Now go to Poptropica
English World

Lesson 8

Can use what I have learnt in Unit 5

Wider World 3
School uniforms

1 **What do you know?**

2 **Listen and read. How many children have got uniforms?**

My name's Clara and I'm from Mexico. In my school we haven't got a uniform. Here I'm wearing a red T-shirt, black trousers and my favourite trainers. They're black and white.

I'm Scott and I'm from the United Kingdom. My school is in Oxford and we've got a uniform. I'm wearing a blue shirt, grey trousers and a blue jacket. I'm wearing my black school shoes.

3 **Write C (Clara), S (Scott), E (Emma) or J (Jiaming).**

1 She isn't wearing a uniform. She's wearing a pink shirt. ☐

2 He's wearing a uniform. He isn't wearing a jacket. ☐

3 She's wearing a T-shirt and trainers. ☐

4 He isn't wearing shorts. He's wearing trousers. ☐

Can understand texts about school uniforms

I'm Emma and I'm from Canada. I'm not wearing a uniform. I'm wearing my favourite jeans and a pink shirt. I love my pink bag!

My name's Jiaming. I'm from China. We've got a uniform in my school. I'm wearing a white shirt, blue shorts, black socks and black trainers.

 Ask and answer.

1 What are you wearing?

2 Are you wearing a uniform?

3 Do you like uniforms?

Tell the Class

6 Sports

do taekwondo

1 ⭐ What do you know?

2 🎧 2:38 Listen and find. What's missing?

play tennis

run

play baseball

ride a bike

3 🎧 2:39 Listen and number.

4 🎧 2:40 Listen and say.

a   b   c   d

e   f   g

play basketball

play football

 5 **Listen and chant. Can the girl swim?**

> I can't swim
> But I can jump!
> Jump, jump, jump!
> I can jump so high.
>
> She can run
> But she can't swim!
> Run, run, run!
> She can run so fast!

 **LOOK!**

I **can** jump and I **can** run.

I **can't** swim but I **can** jump.

She **can** run but she **can't** swim.

 6 **Listen and answer. *True* or *false*?**

1 Katy can ride a bike.

2 Katy can play football.

3 Kim can run fast.

4 Kim can play basketball.

5 Katy can't play tennis.

 7 **Say what you *can* or *can't* do.**

I can run and I can play football.

I can't play tennis but I can swim.

She's very tall, very tall.
Can she play basketball?
Can she? Can she? Can she?
Yes, she can.
Oh, yes, she can. Yes, she can.
She's got strong hands.
Can she catch a ball? (x2)
Can she? Can she? Can she?
Yes, she can.
Oh, yes, she can. (x3)

He's got strong legs.
Can he climb a tree? (x2)
Can he? Can he? Can he?
Yes, he can.
Oh, yes, he can...
Oh, no, he can't.
No, he can't.

catch a ball

climb a tree

 2:47 **LOOK!**

Can he/she play basketball?	Yes, he/she **can**.
	No, he/she **can't**.

9 **Ask and answer.**

Can she play basketball?

Yes, she can.

HOME SCHOOL LINK

10 **Look and read. Then circle the things dolphins can do.**

Dolphins have got a tail, a big nose and a mouth with big teeth but they haven't got legs. Can they walk? No, they can't walk or ride a bike.

Can they swim? Yes, dolphins can swim and jump out of the water but they can't climb trees. They can jump through hoops and catch a ball but they can't play football. I love dolphins!

11 **Listen and correct the sentences.**

12 **Listen and say.**

Ken the kangaroo can catch cakes in the kitchen.

13 **Play the game.**

Can you swim?

Yes, I can.

1
Come and see the Sports Centre. We've got some tifftiff plants.

I'm strong!

Ha, ha!

2
I can play basketball.

Well, I can play tennis.

3
I can swim.

Look! I can ride a bike!

4
Look, I can run.

You're slow! You can't run fast.

SLOW FAST

5
Can you fly?

No, I can't! I haven't got wings!

SLOW FAST

6
Thanks PROD 2!

OK. Come on. Let's find a tifftiff plant.

15   **Act out the story.**

Can understand a simple story / Can act out a story

16 What do you know?

17 Listen and do.

2:54

Keep fit! **Keep healthy!**

1 Stretch your arms up.

2 Bend your knees.

3 Twist your body to the left.

4 Twist your body to the right.

5 Turn around.

18 Read and ask your friend.

How can you keep fit?

You can...

ride a bike.   swim.
play football.   run.
play basketball. jump.
play tennis.   climb trees.

Can you ride a bike?

Yes, I can.

Make a healthy living poster. Talk to a friend.

1 **Think** about healthy living.
2 **Choose** examples of healthy living.
3 **Make** a healthy living poster.
4 **Talk** about your poster.

19   2:56 **Listen and tick (✓) or cross (✗).**

Jake					
Tina					
Simon					
Donna					

20 **Play a guessing game. Look at Activity 19. Ask and answer.**

> He can ride a bike but he can't play baseball.

> Can he play football?

> Yes, he can.

> It's Jake.

21 **Mime a sport. Ask and answer.**

> Can you play basketball?

> Yes, I can!

I **CAN**

I can identify some sports.

I can talk about what people can and can't do.

I can talk about being healthy.

Quiz time!

How healthy are you?

1 Read the questions to your friend and circle Yes or No.

1	Can you play football?	Yes / No
2	Can you run fast?	Yes / No
3	Can you ride a bike?	Yes / No
4	Can you swim?	Yes / No
5	Can you walk to school?	Yes / No
6	Do you like PE?	Yes / No
7	Do you like salad for lunch?	Yes / No
8	Are trainers your favourite shoes?	Yes / No

2 Count the Yes answers and read the results to your friend.

1–2 Yes answers:

Oh, dear! You're not very healthy. Sports are good for you. Walk to school or ride your bike in the park. It's fun!

3–5 Yes answers:

Well done! You're healthy. You play a lot of sports. Keep fit and have fun!

6–8 Yes answers:

Fantastic! You're very healthy. Ask your friends to play sports with you. Have fun!

Now go to Poptropica
English World

7 Food

1 ⭐ **What do you know?**

2 🎧 3:01 **Listen and find. What's missing?**

cucumbers
peas
plums
potatoes
oranges
strawberries
tomatoes
beans

3 🎧 3:02 **Listen and number.**

4 🎧 3:03 **Listen and say.**

a
b
c
d
e
f
g
h

Can identify some fruit and vegetables

5 3:04 **Listen and chant.
Circle the food words.**

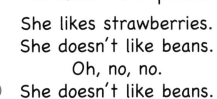  

He likes peas.
He doesn't like plums.
Oh, no, no.
He doesn't like plums.

She likes strawberries.
She doesn't like beans.
Oh, no, no.
She doesn't like beans.

 3:05 **LOOK!**

He/She	**likes**	strawberries.
	doesn't like	

6 3:06 **Listen and answer.** *True* or *false*?

1 PROD 2 likes peas.

2 PROD 2 likes plums.

3 PROD 1 doesn't like tomatoes.

4 PROD 1 likes strawberries.

7   **Look and say.**

He doesn't
like plums.

He likes
tomatoes.

8 **Listen and sing.**

3:08 / 3:09

Does she like carrots?
Yes, she does.
Yes, she does.
No, I don't! No, I don't!
Yuck, yuck, yuck.
Does she like peaches?
No, she doesn't.
No, she doesn't.
Yes, I do! Yes, I do!
Yum, yum, yum.

Does he like peas?
Yes, he does.
Yes, he does.
No, I don't! No, I don't!
Yuck, yuck, yuck.
Does he like potatoes?
No, he doesn't.
No, he doesn't.
Yes, I do! Yes, I do!
Yum, yum, yum.

carrots

peaches

3:10  **LOOK!**

9 **Ask and answer.**

Does he/she **like** potatoes?

Yes, he/she **does**.

No, he/she **doesn't**.

Does she like peaches?

Yes, she does.

 HOME SCHOOL LINK

10 **Look and read. Which food does Lisa like?**

Lisa Martin Astronaut

Reporter:	Hello, Lisa Martin. Do you have breakfast in space?
Lisa:	Yes, I do, breakfast, lunch and dinner.
Reporter:	Do you like bananas for breakfast?
Lisa:	Yes, I do. Yum!
Reporter:	Do you like plums and strawberries?
Lisa:	I like plums, but I don't like strawberries.
Reporter:	Do you like beans and potatoes for dinner?
Lisa:	I like beans but I don't like potatoes. Yuck!
Reporter:	Thank you, Lisa.

11 **Listen and answer.**
3:11

SOUNDS FUN!

12 **Listen and say.**
3:12

Big **B**ob likes **b**reakfast, **b**ananas, **b**eans and **b**read.

Pretty **P**at likes **p**eas, **p**eaches and **p**lums. Yum, yum, yum.

13 **Play the game.**

Do you like peaches?

No, I don't.

15   **Act out the story.**

16 **What do you know?**

17 3:16 **Listen and read. Then put the foods in the correct place.**

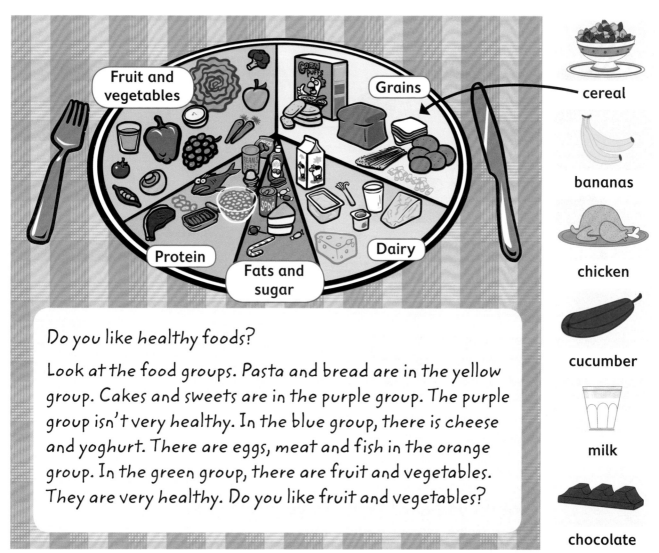

Fruit and vegetables

Grains

cereal

bananas

chicken

cucumber

milk

chocolate

Protein

Fats and sugar

Dairy

Do you like healthy foods?

Look at the food groups. Pasta and bread are in the yellow group. Cakes and sweets are in the purple group. The purple group isn't very healthy. In the blue group, there is cheese and yoghurt. There are eggs, meat and fish in the orange group. In the green group, there are fruit and vegetables. They are very healthy. Do you like fruit and vegetables?

18 **Say the word.
Find the food group.**

Milk.

Blue group!

PROJECT

**Make a healthy food plate.
Talk to a friend.**

1 **Think** about healthy food.
2 **Draw** or find examples of healthy food.
3 **Make** a healthy food plate.
4 **Talk** about your food plate.

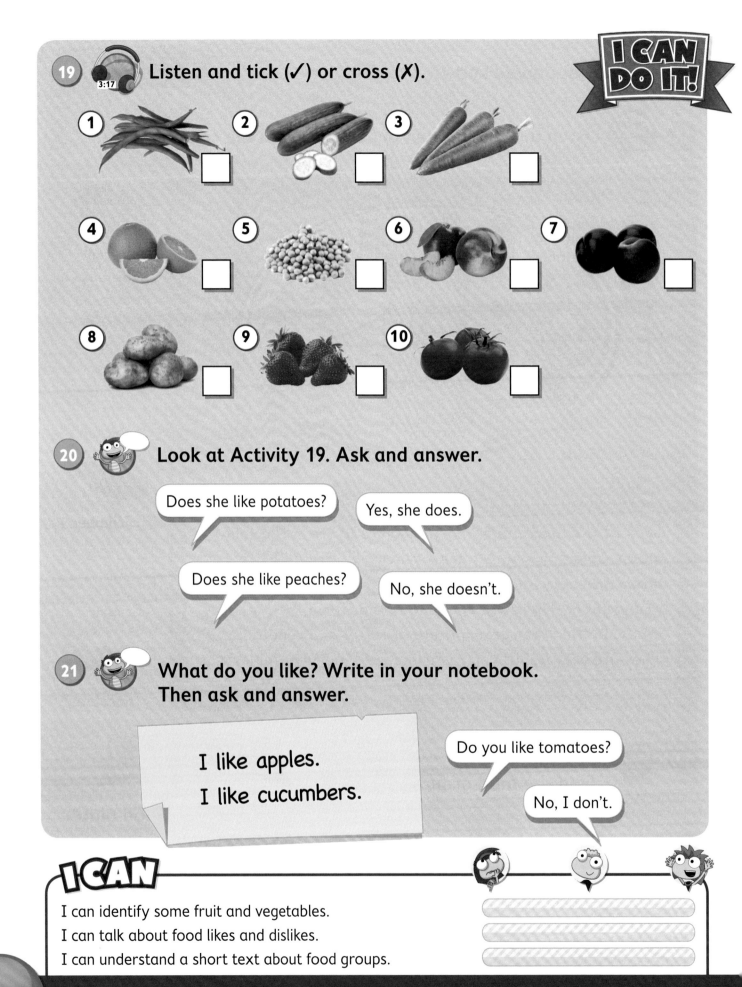

19 Listen and tick (✓) or cross (✗).

1 □
2 □
3 □
4 □
5 □
6 □
7 □
8 □
9 □
10 □

20 Look at Activity 19. Ask and answer.

Does she like potatoes?

Yes, she does.

Does she like peaches?

No, she doesn't.

21 What do you like? Write in your notebook.
Then ask and answer.

I like apples.
I like cucumbers.

Do you like tomatoes?

No, I don't.

I CAN

I can identify some fruit and vegetables.
I can talk about food likes and dislikes.
I can understand a short text about food groups.

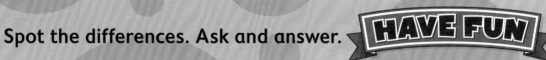

22 Spot the differences. Ask and answer.

A Alfie

B Bob

Does Bob like carrots?

Yes, he does.

Does Alfie like tomatoes?

No, he doesn't.

23  Write about the differences in your notebook.

Picture A:

Alfie likes cucumbers.

Picture B:

Bob doesn't like cucumbers.

Now go to Poptropica
English World

Wider World 4
Food around the world

1 **What do you know?**

2 **Listen and read. How many children like chicken?**

3:18

1

I'm Andrea. I'm from Argentina. I don't like potatoes but I like meat. My favourite dinner is *asado* or barbecue.

asado

My name's Zeki and I'm from Turkey. These fantastic pastries have got nuts in them. They aren't very healthy but I also like fruit. I like chicken but I don't like fish.

2

pastries

3 **Match.**

1	Berta	**a**	likes chicken but he doesn't like fish.
2	Kay	**b**	likes pizza and chocolate ice cream.
3	Zeki	**c**	likes meat but she doesn't like potatoes.
4	Andrea	**d**	likes rice and peas but doesn't like pumpkin soup.

Can understand texts about food likes and dislikes

3

My name's Kay. I'm from Jamaica. My favourite lunch is jerk chicken with rice and peas. Yum! I also like meat patties but I don't like pumpkin soup.

jerk chicken

meat patties

4

I'm Berta and I'm from Italy. My favourite dinner is pizza with cheese and tomatoes. I also like chocolate ice cream.

ice cream

4  **Ask and answer.**

1 Does Andrea like *asado*?

2 Does Zeki like pastries?

3 Does Kay like pumpkin soup?

4 Does Berta like ice cream?

5 What's your favourite food?

Tell the Class

8 Things we do

1 What do you know?

2 3:19 Listen and find. What's missing?

listening to music

3 3:20 Listen and number.

 **a**

 **b**

 **c**

 **d**

 **e**

 **f**

 **g**

 **h**

reading

drinking

eating

dancing

4 3:21 Listen and say.

70 Lesson 1

Can identify some actions and activities

sleeping

doing homework

cleaning

5 3:23 **Listen and chant.**
Point at the pictures.

What are you doing?
I'm drinking, I'm drinking.
What are you doing?
I'm cleaning, I'm cleaning.
What are you doing?
I'm sleeping, I'm sleeping.

 3:24 **LOOK!**

| What **are** you | do**ing**? | **I'm** | sleep**ing**. |

6 3:25 **Listen and answer. *True* or *False*?**

1 He's doing his homework.

2 She's cleaning.

3 She's eating.

4 He's sleeping.

7 **Mime and answer.**

What are you doing?

I'm reading.

Lesson 2

Listen and sing.

Are you sleeping?
No, I'm not.
Are you jumping?
Yes, I am.
I'm jumping very high,
I can touch the sky.
Are you sleeping?
No, I'm not.
Are you walking?
Yes, I am.
I'm walking in the park,
With my friend, Mark.

Are you sleeping?
No, I'm not.
Are you running?
Yes, I am.
I'm running on the grass,
Very, very fast.
Are you sleeping?
No, I'm not.
Are you swimming?
Yes, I am.
I'm swimming in a pool,
It's very, very cool.

walking

running

jumping

swimming

LOOK!

3:29

| **Are** you jump**ing**? | Yes, I **am**. |
| | No, I'**m not**. |

9 **Ask and answer.**

Are you swimming?

Yes, I am.

HOME SCHOOL LINK

Can identify more actions and activities

10 Read and find four mistakes.

 READING **8**

Dear Granny and Grandad,

Hello from Spain! It's sunny and cold here. We're at the swimming pool. I'm eating an ice cream. Tim is reading in the pool and Dad is listening to music. It's fun!

Lots of love,
Tracy

Mr & Mrs Jones
2 London Road
Weymouth
D58 3RF
England

 **11** Listen and say. Who is it?

SOUNDS FUN!

12 Listen and say.

The swan is swimm**ing** and eat**ing** and drink**ing** and sleep**ing**.

13 Play the game.

Are you jumping?

Yes, I am!

Talk about the pictures. Then listen and read.

 15 **Act out the story.**

8

16 **What do you know?**

17 **Listen and read. Then write B = Balloon or R = Rocket.**
3:37

Flying machines

This is a hot-air balloon. It's flying on hot air. It hasn't got wings but it can fly. It isn't very fast. A pilot is flying the balloon.

What's this rocket doing? It's flying very high. It's big but it can fly in space. Three astronauts are in this rocket.

1 It isn't very fast. ☐	2 It can fly very high. ☐
3 It's flying on hot air. ☐	4 A pilot is flying it. ☐
5 It's flying to space. ☐	6 Astronauts are in it. ☐

PROJECT

Make a flying machine mobile. Talk to a friend.

1 **Think** about flying machines.
2 **Choose** and draw a flying machine on a card.
3 **Cut** out your flying machine and hang it up.
4 **Talk** about your flying machine.

18   **Listen and match.**

1	eat	**a**	to music
2	drink	**b**	homework
3	listen	**c**	the bath
4	play	**d**	milk
5	read	**e**	a book
6	do	**f**	to school
7	walk	**g**	lunch
8	clean	**h**	basketball

19 **Choose actions from Activity 18. Mime, ask and answer.**

Are you eating lunch?

Yes, I am.

20 **Draw a picture of you doing an action in your notebook. Ask and answer.**

What are you doing?

I'm walking to school.

I can identify some actions and activities.
I can talk about what people are doing.
I can understand short texts about flying machines.

(21) **How many sentences can you make in five minutes? Look and write in your notebook. Then say.**

playing basketball   reading   sleeping

I'm listening to music in the living room.

I'm sleeping in the bedroom.

Now go to Poptropica English World

HAVE FUN
8

Lesson 8

Can use what I have learnt in Unit 8

Goodbye

1 🎧 3:40 **Listen, find and number.**

2 🎧 3:41 **Listen. Who is missing?**

Can identify the story characters

Christmas

 1 Listen, find and say.

 2 Listen and sing.

> Happy Christmas, Thank you Santa.
> It's Christmas Day today.
> Happy Christmas, Thank you Santa.
> Let's go and play.
> Look at the pretty lights
> And presents under the tree.
> There are cards and Christmas stockings
> For you and for me.

 3 Listen and answer.

1 Has Anna got a blue bike?   2 Has Mike got a car?

3 Are there sweets in the Christmas stockings?   4 Has Mum got a dress?

5 Has Dad got a book?

Festival

Can sing a song about Christmas

Easter

 **1** 3:47 **Listen, find and say.**

 2 3:48 / 3:49 **Listen and sing.**

> There goes the Easter bunny,
> He's hiding chocolate eggs.
> There's one under the bag
> And there's one in the tree.
> They're tied with pretty ribbon,
> They're yummy and sweet.
> Can you find the Easter eggs?
> A yummy chocolate treat!

ribbon

Easter bunny

Easter basket

Easter egg

 3 3:50 **Listen and answer.**

1 Where's the blue egg?

2 Is the pink egg under the tree?

3 Where's the pink egg?

Can sing a song about Easter

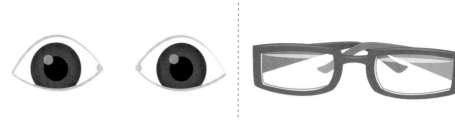

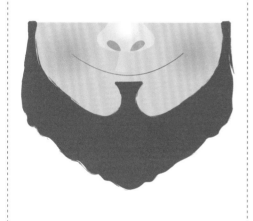
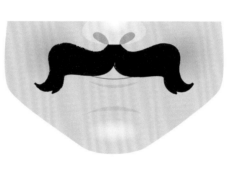

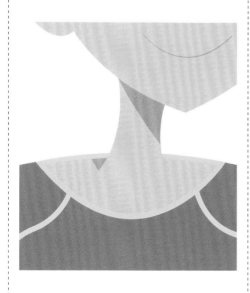

Name:

Name:

Name:

Name:

Name:

Name:

Name:

Name:

Name:

Name:

Name:

Name:

Name:

Name:

Name:

Name:

Name:

Name:

Name:

Name:

Name:

Name:

Name:

Name:

Name:

Name:

Name:

Name:

Name:

Name:

Name:

Name:

Name:

Name:

Name:

Name:

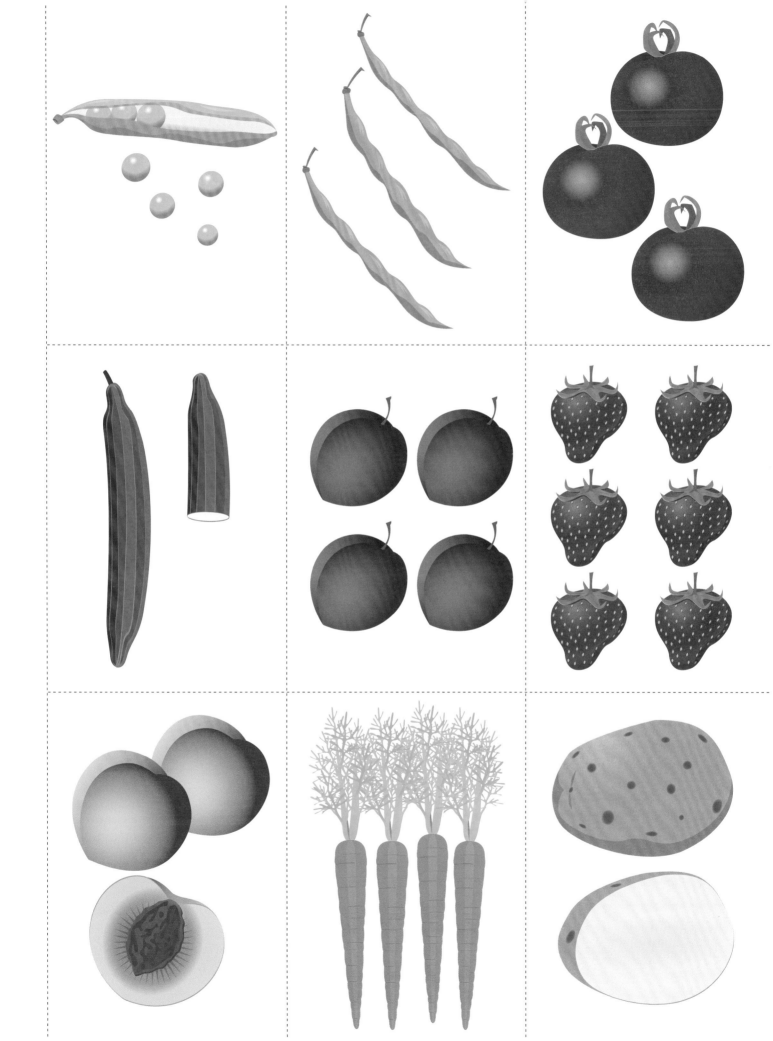

Name:

Name:

Name:

Name:

Name:

Name:

Name:

Name:

Name: